The Tale of Two Dolphins

(When my sister died suddenly)

Written by ***Sarah Fitzgerald***
Illustrated by ***Kate Gallé***

Brambles's Trust

Bramble's Trust is a charity offering bereavement support to children and young people in North Worcestershire and the surrounding areas. It was founded by Liz and Steve Fitzgerald, as a result of what they found in the aftermath of the M40 minibus accident in November 1993. The writing of this book has helped to inspire the formation of Bramble's Trust.

First Edition 1998   Second Edition 1999

Published by Bramble's Press, Bannut Tree House, Lye Head, Bewdley, Worcs, DY12 2UW
Printed by T Snape & Company Limited, Bolton's Court, Preston, Lancs., PR1 3TY

HARDBACK ISBN 0 9534476 1 8
PAPERBACK ISBN 0 9534476 2 6
(First Edition ISBN 0 9534476 0 X)

From the net revenues generated by the sale of these Impressions of this book, 60% will be donated to Bramble's Trust (Charity Number 1070002), 20% to the Whale and Dolphin Conservation Society (WDCS – Charity Number 1014705) and 20% to Acorns Children's Hospice (Charity Number 700859).

THE TALE OF TWO DOLPHINS

This book belongs to

____

____

____

Remembering with love Claire and all of her friends who died on the M40 in November 1993:

Louise, Anna, Charlotte, Charlene, Adele, Nicola, Ruth, Fiona, Katie, Richard, James and their teacher, Eleanor Fry.

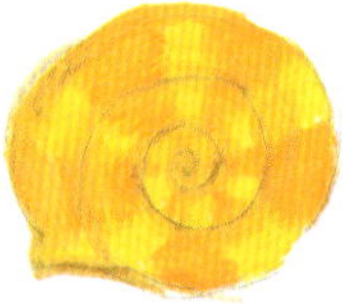

Sarah and Kate would especially like to thank Phil Smith and John O'Neill for all of their help.

Foreword by Sarah

This is about when my sister died and how I felt. I knew my relatives and friends cared, but I felt they couldn't really understand. Claire was very close to me.

If you are reading this book after something has happened to you, you must realise you are not alone. This book is for you and me.

Choose someone you are close to and read this book together.

It was hard to write and it will be hard to read, because our feelings about those we love loads are hard to think about, but we need to do it. They will always love us too.

I really hope this story will help you.

Love

Sarah

PS A special thanks to my friend Phil, from Acorns, who helped me be strong enough to write this story, and to Katie who illustrated it.

THE TALE OF TWO DOLPHINS

Claire and Sarah were two dolphins who lived in the sea near the coast of Ireland in a place called Dingle. Claire was five years older than Sarah and was a bit bossy. They used to play chasing fish and jumping high out of the water. Claire always seemed to be the fastest and be able to jump the highest. Both Claire and Sarah used to get on their parents' nerves by messing around doing silly things, but their parents loved them anyway even when they were bad.

Sarah was a bit jealous of Claire because she used to beat her at nearly everything; everything that is except catching fish. Claire was not as good at catching fish as Sarah because she had a long nose that was not very good for this job, and besides she did not have enough patience. As all fishermen know, catching fish takes patience - and that is something that Sarah had that Claire did not.

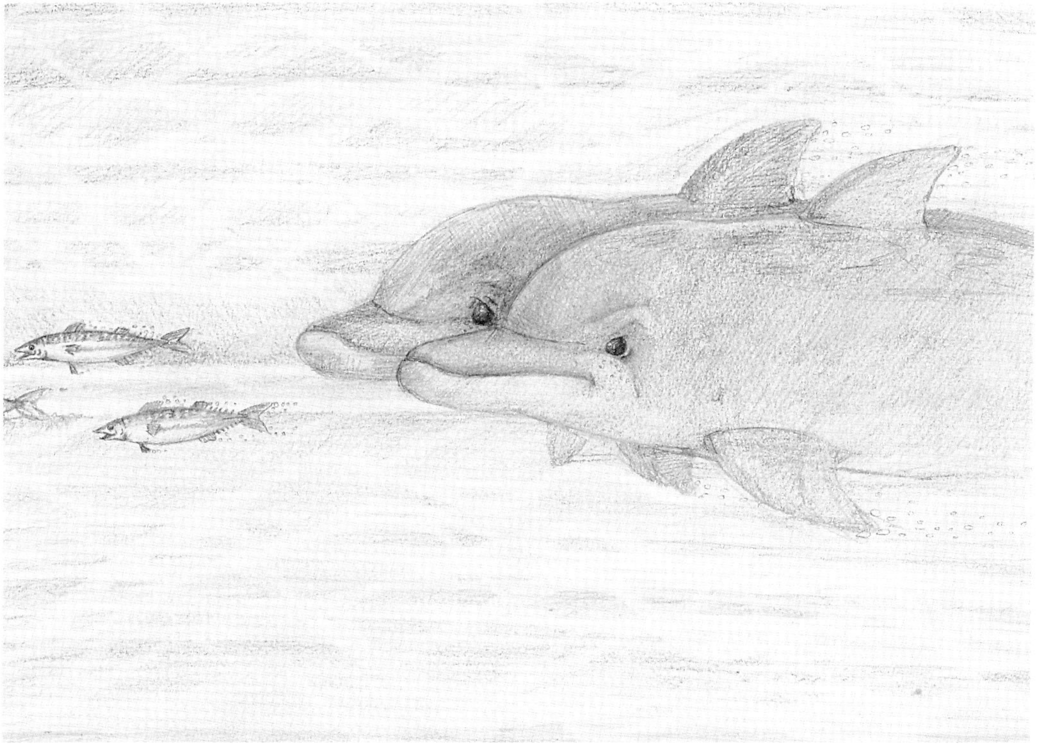

One windy day Claire and Sarah went further out to sea than they usually did, because the water was murky and they couldn't see where they were going. Claire decided to play her jumping and racing game, pretending that she wasn't afraid, but Sarah was frightened and felt very lost. Sarah knew that her Mum and Dad would be worried because they were only supposed to be fishing in the bay.

Suddenly Sarah heard the noise of a boat engine and felt the touch of the scraggy nets on her body. She was frightened and swam faster than she had ever swum before until she escaped from the surrounding suffocating nets. Then she called out for Claire who she thought must have escaped too, after all Claire was the fastest. She kept crying out, but there was no reply. Sarah felt alone and worried.

Her parents were distraught so they went out searching for their daughters. By now the sea had calmed and just before the sun went down they found Sarah. She was crying and could not talk to them.

They took her back home and on the way they met a tuna fish who had almost been caught by the fishermen. He told them about the fishing boat and that he had heard Sarah calling out for Claire. He thought that Claire must have been caught and killed. Mum and Dad cried a lot but Sarah went away on her own.

For all the next week she kept herself to herself and spent most of her time in a secret place in the bay; she didn't eat much, she didn't want to play except by herself. She kept thinking about Claire and about the things they used to do together. She felt locked away from the world in her dreams of how things used to be.

One day another dolphin called Laura came and found Sarah in her secret hiding place in the bay. Sarah told her about her sister being caught. They spent the rest of the day together, laughing, crying, joking and playing. She felt that she could talk to Laura about her feelings.

Now Sarah wanted to talk to her Mum and Dad, she wanted a hug. Sarah went home and spent ages hugging and crying with her Mum and Dad. She felt safe in their flippers. Their tears joined together as one in the ocean. Mum was the first to break the silence. “It was okay to cry,” she said, “Look, even your Dad’s crying.” Dad smiled that big smile that Sarah loved. During the next few weeks they tried to have some fun but it was hard without Claire.

Then one day Dad said, "Let's go to the place where Claire was killed."

He said he would feel close to Claire there and Sarah and Mum agreed. So they went.

As they got near Sarah began to feel anxious and worried because it felt like a scary place. She went all numb. So numb she didn't notice the fish she liked to eat go past her nose.

Over the next few months and years Sarah went there alone, sometimes with her Mum and Dad and sometimes with her very special friends. She always thought about Claire when she went there and she felt that Claire was near to her. The more she went the more it stopped being scary. Sarah knew that she would never forget the greatest sister in the world.

The End

I have started to learn to be happy because I know that Claire would not want me to be down all the time. She would want me to take all the opportunities life offers me and have fun, because she always liked us to do stuff together anyway. So I just want to carry these things on, for me and for Claire.

Sarah

age 13

About Dolphins

- There are 27 species of dolphins living in the sea in different parts of the world.
- There are also 5 species of river dolphin. River dolphins are comical-looking: some are bubblegum pink, and have very bad eyesight. Sadly, they are very rare.
- The bottlenose dolphin is one of the largest and most common dolphins It is also the best known. Flipper, the star of several films, was a bottlenose dolphin.
- Bottlenose dolphins can swim very fast. They are real acrobats and seem to enjoy leaping clear out of the water.
- Dolphins are not fish, they are mammals, just like us! They are warm blooded and feed their young with milk. Dolphins need air to survive, so they come to the surface regularly to breathe.
- Dolphins mainly eat fish which they catch using a form of sonar known as "echolocation". This helps them to locate their prey, even in murky or dark waters. Bats use a similar method to catch moths at night.
- The smallest dolphin is called the Hector's dolphin which is only found off the coast of New Zealand. It is only 1.2 metres long and weighs about 30 kg. About 3000 Hector's dolphins weigh the same as the largest whale, the blue whale.
- Dolphins seem to like people - there are many stories over the years of dolphins coming to the rescue of shipwrecked sailors, or drowning people.
- The Whale and Dolphin Conservation Society (WDCS) is a charity working hard to help whales and dolphins all over the world.

This information about dolphins is courtesy of the WDCS.